"It's no good messing with an invincible man."

Invincible Man

John Danen

Published by John Danen, 2024.

INVINCIBLE MAN

First edition. June 10, 2024.

Copyright © 2024 John Danen.

ISBN: 979-8227321725

Written by John Danen.

Table of Contents

Introduction. 1

Where does cursed love come from? 3

The illusion of love. 5

The hardness of being born a man. 7

The life of man. 9

Statistics on men. 13

The terrible example of a man at war. 14

The trauma of the first girlfriend. 19

The best woman I know. 21

Masculinity. 23

Clothing. 25

Elimination. 27

Some good men. 29

Some bad women. 30

Some good women. 31

The most important chapter of all the books. 32

Meditation to feel the fucking power. 40

Never give up. 41

The invincible man and love 43

The invincible man and death. 44

Transcending seduction. 46

Evil. 47

Women. 48

Invincible man phrases. 50

Ten tips to govern your life 52

The brutality of men. 53

Pain. 54

Sex, sex, sex and don't forget the violence. 56

You can't be defeated even in death. 58

The invincible man is addicted to victory. 60

Building the invincible man. 61

Invincible man statements 63
Shackleton... 66
Exercise to become an invincible man............................... 68
Feeling like the invincible man. 70

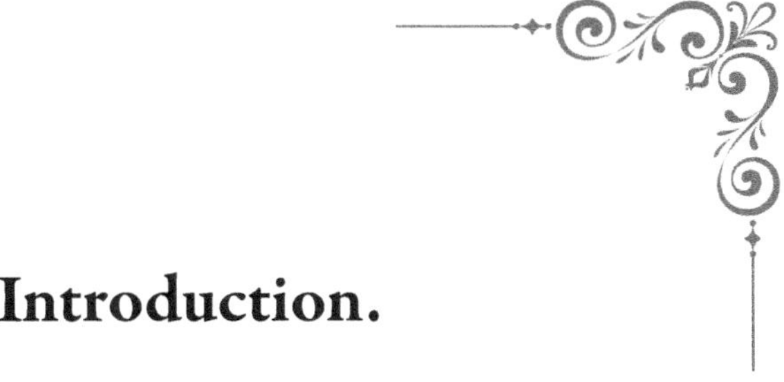

Introduction.

I make this book to help men and also women. For you to see the dangers of being a romantic, weak, needy person. Someone who prioritizes love above all else. Instead it is better to become an invincible man.

This is going to be a book that could cause you a lot of pain, it is brutally hard. If you are sensitive, I ask you not to read it, or you may be traumatized by what appears here.

But if you have the courage to want to know the truth, this is the book for you.

Misdirected love **can kill**. Of course, it is very beautiful, and if we were all good, it should be what we should be looking for, a precious love. But, this concept that some people have idealized of love in their head, makes them commit all kinds of barbarities against them and against them, it also makes them suffer a real hell. Love kills men and women. That is why I am writing this book, to make you realize how bad things can happen to you if you are naive, if you believe that love is greater than anything, and you seek it above your personal wellbeing.

With misdirected love, everyone suffers. I am going to do this book from a man's perspective, telling all the misfortunes that can happen to you, man, but I could also do another book from a woman's perspective, telling how men are bad and give them a shitty life. I'm sorry, I'm not going to do this second vision, not because I don't consider it fair, which is fair and they also suffer a lot, it's simply because I'm not on the other side, and I don't know in depth their sufferings.

So I ask someone else to write that other part where women suffer for love. Suffice it with this part that I do know to horrify everyone, and prevent men and women from suffering. I want both to be very careful when they get together in a serious relationship. If we all value ourselves above this idyllic love, many problems will be avoided.

It is not machismo or feminism that I defend, but having a head and not falling into cursed loves that ruin the lives of an enormous number of people.

This is a book for your personal defense, so that you know what women and men do in love, how they often use and manipulate us. It is not a love book, it is a book that tells in a realistic way how are the personal relationships between men and women in today's world. I could have called it toxic love, but I am going to call it "**the invincible man**" because it is more positive and empowering.

Loves are not toxic, they are cursed because what they call love, many times, turns into something horrendous, which destroys people forever.

Man, because of his weakness and natural goodness, often falls into these cursed loves and is terribly punished. Also because of his excess of aggressiveness and self-control he commits terrible acts.

I hope that with this book you will become an invincible man who does not fall in cursed loves, nor suffer, nor cry. A man above good and evil who has gone through everything, and, finally, has risen invincible.

Where does cursed love come from?

Cursed love comes from weakness, from the belief that love is the most important thing, and that for which you have to suffer and fight, even above your personal well-being. Cursed love comes from being emotionally dependent, soft and sensitive, fighting for this love beyond what would be advisable. You have to know how to stop, you have to know how to value yourself and say no to the other person, you have to know how to abandon relationships that bring nothing, well if they bring, they bring suffering and unhappiness.

Many times we blame women for our ills, as if they were bad and did evil to us, it is not so, it is us who by being soft we give them total power over our feelings. This happens because of our kindness sometimes, sometimes it is innocence, sometimes it is clearly weakness and dependence.

Because of our conception of idyllic love, women may seem bad to us, and yes, it is true, they can be very bad, but most of the time they are neither good nor bad. They adapt to what you are, if you are soft they will be very hard, if you are hard they will be soft. They adapt to complement.

In general they do not like the soft man, the sensitive and romantic man, they like the man who makes himself respected, who sets limits, who is hard, that is the most coveted man.

A man who cries is rejected by any woman because this is forbidden for men, who despite suffering a lot, but a lot, is not allowed. They can cry for anything. If a man cries in front of a woman, he is practically discarded, because you have to be tough no matter what happens to you because you are a man.

We have to do our bit so that everything goes well, and at least try to be someone who respects himself and does not fall into toxic relationships where we will have everything to lose.

In love **you can't win**, only if you find a perfect relationship you will be happy more or less, but you will also suffer a lot of problems. At most, there are those who make themselves respected, who also find a very good partner, and who in turn, they are good, those few, get to tie. The great majority loses in love, sometimes both men and women lose, this is rare, in 99.99999% of the times we men lose, we are the weak ones in love.

The normal result is 18-0

I hope that with this book you can tie the game, winning is very difficult and practically no one in the history of mankind has been able to do it.

Casanova and 10 others succeeded. To win you should enjoy more than suffer, and as soon as you give importance to one, it will weaken you and cause you terrible sufferings that you won't forget even if you pick up 100 more.

Only the invincible man achieves what nobody achieves and wins by the minimum a few times in a century. Only 1 in ten million draws.

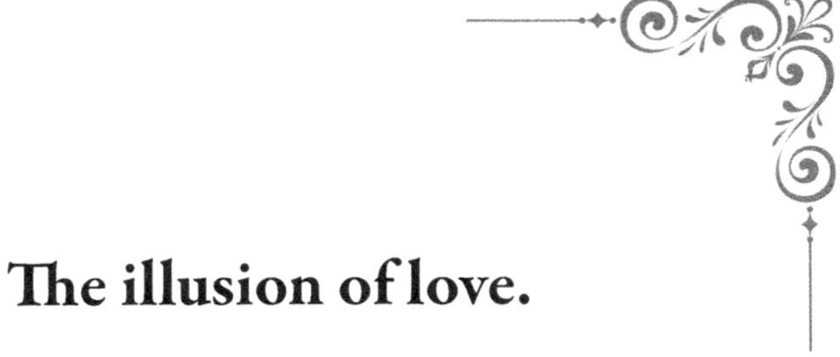

The illusion of love.

Because of the illusion of love that gets into our heads, we lose years, and even entire lives dedicated to the search for a love that is difficult to achieve, or that really does not exist. As Manson said "I am not a slave to a God that does not exist", and it is true, Cupid does not exist, there is no God of love to pay obeisance to. When people realize that love does not exist, or at least that it is very difficult to find it, they suffer terribly.

Some become violent precisely against the person who is the object of their love, because their frustration for not getting this love, or for not being reciprocated as they want, makes them commit all kinds of savage actions, which destroy their lives and those of other people.

From love one can pass to hatred and from hatred to pain, and then nothing can be solved, because things have been done that are so despicable that there is no possible consolation.

If people did not have such a strong emotional dependence, this search for love at all costs doing whatever it takes, and, as soon as they detect that they are not being reciprocated as they should, they would break their relationships, everything would be much better.

But from scarcity comes fear, and from fear comes pain. He who is a formal man is a dangerous man, for he is often obsessed with his partner and does not see beyond that relationship.

However, the seducer goes around accepting that many do not treat him well, accepting that many despise him, knowing that he will not be reciprocated practically never, and not giving importance to anything.

The seducer is hard, really hard, that's why, because the seducer is hard, he is looking for his own enjoyment, to have a good time, and he will not hurt anyone.

But beware! The formal man, the soft man who is dedicated to only one woman and who is obsessed with that relationship, can be dangerous.

I'm not going to say that everyone has to be seductive either, but at least that they respect themselves and have the balls to break up the relationship they're in if it doesn't make them happy.

There can always be another girl who will give you a better life than the one you are with who does not satisfy you. Leave her and go on your way, this book is also valid to avoid violent crimes of macho dye that horrify people in society.

So even though I'm going to tell a lot of wild stories, what I hope with all this is to make people aware to do good, and good many times, is to break relationships and respect yourself, let's start!

The hardness of being
born a man.

If you have had the misfortune of being born a man like me, I have terrible news for you, being a man is dangerous, dangerous no, very dangerous. Men have much more testosterone which incites us to violence, we also run infinite risks. Many of these risks we run are produced by looking for a woman, or fighting for a love, or defending someone. It is not for nothing that men live seven years less than women. We take less care of ourselves, we take much more risks, we like speed, we like in a certain way and in some circumstances we also like violence, wild motor sports, in short, when our heart beats for the adrenaline of emotion we feel alive, and that is dangerous for us and for others.

You have to accept this hard and crude truth, **women are not bad**, what happens is that you are soft and demand a kindness that many times they cannot give. They can't give it because they have been programmed that way for millions of years. They can only give a small kindness to the one they consider their partner, and this in the best of cases, for everyone else there is coldness and distrustful behavior. They protect their own and are hostile to the rest most of the time. Once the woman opens up, that is to say, conquered, she becomes good, unless you are excessively soft, which she will compensate by becoming colder and

harder.

In general it must also be said that, in themselves, they are already much colder and meaner, but it is not their fault, they have been programmed this way, as I said before, it is their adaptation to survive. Not having physical strength, they have developed cunning, and they are light years ahead of us in terms of power in this quality. This can often be interpreted as evil, but they are like that, it is not their fault. Don't complain about how mean the woman is, because that's the way she has to be, complain about how soft and weak you are.

You are a man, and if you aspire to be an invincible man, you can't complain about anything.

Complaining is for failures. Invincible men never complain.

"Man is hard on the outside and soft on the inside, woman is weak on the outside and hard on the inside."

We men have countless accidents and violent deaths due to excess testosterone, yes I know. That's how it must be here too. Everything is perfect just the way it is. There is no complaint, no grief. Invincible men accept everything that comes their way, without complaint.

The life of man.

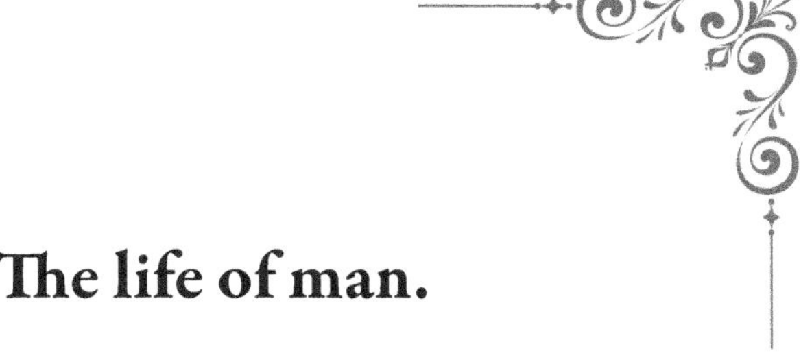

I am going to tell how the man's life is from his birth. In the beginning he is a very kind, innocent and candid being, whose only reference is his mother. She is the one who protects him from everything bad in the world, the one who gives him affection and love. This affection and love that he will never find again, or what he will find will be a very low love. This affection and love that he will hopefully find will be a cheap copy of this maternal love. When he has already built his invincible version he doesn't need it either, he is an invincible man who is happy with nothing, he is very hard, he has enough to be happy with himself. But now as a young man he is weak and fragile.

When the young man starts to like girls, he usually receives a very hard blow. He has everything to do, he has to build his personality, he has to toughen up to be able to compete on equal terms with them.

So this poor boy goes around doing the natural thing, falling in love and being good, loving and romantic with the wonderful and beautiful girls. This happens because society, family, schools, parents, movies, everything, leads him towards romanticism and idyllic love which is the goal to achieve.

The boy thinks and feels, but those thoughts and feelings are not truly his own, they have been inculcated by this society. That is why until he gets rid of this old, badly programmed self, he cannot succeed in love. This self that is programmed by others, the child associates it with himself, and believes that it is his true self, but it is not. The child thinks and feels this way because he is immersed in the dominant current of thought, because he cannot get out of it, because that is what he knows, that is why the child, one hundred percent of the time, becomes a soft, sensitive and dependent person looking for love.

So he goes out in search of love and fails completely, since they often if not almost always repay his kindness with contempt, lies, and humiliation.

This can trigger three things in the male mind:

- Number one I think almost everyone has gone through it, it's about a **hatred for women**, who will be seen as evil beings that cause all our problems.
- Number two is another possibility, which consists of accepting them as they are with resignation, and **continuing to look for love** like good boys until the end.
- Option three is for you to become an **invincible man**, which I will explain throughout this book.

I will first analyze **option number two**.

Those who have continued to look for love find a manipulated love, a love that is not true, a love that comes from their weakness, and they are all enslaved without any mercy by women. Thus they truncate their lives and instead of being happy seducing and having a good time, they are bitter, often putting up with a despot woman, who humiliates them and treats them quite badly.

They do everything to protect the family, and in short, they are great heroes too, heroes who sacrifice their lives so that their children may prosper. The greatest of these sacrifices is putting up with his wife, who most of the time is a woman who became mean and hard when she saw how good and soft he was. Other times she is semi-good, the point is that she will be as good as she can to him, because he is her man, whether she likes him very much or not, she chose him and now she takes him for good. He has committed to form a family with her and therefore she must treat him the best she can, even so this man will clearly lose out in love and deserves our commiseration.

In 70% of the occasions, well this is a number that I put a little randomly and I do not have the precise data, but I estimate that it is something like this; marriages fail, and afterwards, these men, good or bad or whatever they are, suffer in their flesh, in all its crudeness, the unjust laws that deprive them of their children, and of more than half of their goods. Many suffer an ordeal of trials, appeals, and are ruined by lawyers. All for trying to see their usually ungrateful children, who are totally manipulated by their mothers, with the approval of the whole of the biemensante society.

In the most extreme cases they go crazy and do barbarities. Some commit suicide, others kill the woman, but these are extreme cases that are not normal. What is normal is to rebuild their lives and fall back into the same traps, all for continuing to believe in love, a love as I said before, in which you will never win, you will always lose, and at most, but very, very much, a draw. They always lose by a landslide.

This love, if you swallow all her demands, will restrict your freedom. She will forbid you to be a man, to go with other women, to sleep with others, which is what nature really wants for you. This marriage is made for you to take care of your family, but once this is done, you do not find happiness, neither in the first, nor in the second nor in the fifth, they are all more of the same. Illusion at the beginning, suffering in the middle, and tremendous disappointment at the end.

These men who marry never succeed in love; on the contrary, they fail terribly.

Many do not even get married because they suffer so much from rejections and failures that they do not make it, since they fall into deep depressions caused by these misfortunes, and they do not fly again.

Option one in which many fall into, is to hate women, this has happened to all of us when we were kids, when we did not understand anything and did not know, now that we are mature and know we realize that although they appear to be very bad, in reality they are as they should be, because that is how nature created them, because they survived better, because by developing the cunning they could cope with the hard life that they also had. So I ask for your own good that you stop complaining about women, that is a failure, a total loser.

Option three is to stop hating them or pandering to them and become **an invincible man,** that's the real path, path number three.

We men are alone, nobody helps us because we are already men, we are not children or women, we are men and we must solve our own things.

Statistics on men.

It is no coincidence that so many people want to change their sex to female. As I said before, being a man is dangerous. Most of the data that reflect all these statistics come from our own fault, from our impulsiveness and aggressiveness, but there are these devastating statistics.

Men suffer 4.3 times more deaths on the road, i.e., for every woman who dies, more than 4 men do.

Men go to war and account for 99% of the casualty figures. For every woman killed in battle there are 99 men. No one here is calling for parity?

Men commit suicide more than four times more often than women.

Women initiate 70% of divorces.

Men are used to putting up with it, they are the ones who receive most of the violence. Most violence is from men to men.

Nora Vincent is an activist and feminist writer. This woman did an experiment for eighteen months, which consisted of pretending to be a man. She suffered so much that she fell into depression. According to her, her life as a man was brutally difficult and hard. She said that she admired men and that our life was much, much harder than that of women. She would know.

The terrible example of a man at war.

This is an example I'm going to make up, but reality can be like that, and even harsher.

Our protagonist is a 28-year-old man who has been forcibly enlisted to defend his country, he had no military training, but he had to do it because only men defend their homeland in wars. He is a man of mobilization age, so, in order not to incur the death penalty for deserting, here he is on the front lines.

The temperature is sixteen degrees below zero, the man is not too well equipped for the cold, as provisions are scarce. He shivers and shivers most of the time. He has not eaten anything solid for two days, only a sachet soup that he barely heats on a small stove and that he shares with two other fighters.

At night he cries and remembers his home, his wife, and his two small children. He doesn't hear from them, no letters arrive at the front. He hopes that perhaps she has escaped and is now safely in another country, a warm and safe place.

Every night he thinks about them and what his life would be like if he wasn't fighting for his country.

Three long months pass without anything important happening. There is only the tedium of standing on the front line waiting for the enemy to approach. But the enemy does not deign to show up. This gives you a little hope that maybe he will never show up, and you can return in one piece to your home, if you are still standing. Also maybe he could get his family back if this war were to end soon. He dreams of embracing his wife and children. He prays every day for their well-being. He thinks, "I wish I could come home and find my family waiting for me." The soldier thinks that he wishes he could communicate with them, and sometimes fantasizes about the best news, that the war is over and he can be reunited with his family wherever he is.

One fateful day at 5:47 a.m. a heavy bombardment begins on his position. The bombs burst his eardrums and he bleeds from them, the pain is intense, the noise infernal.

He huddles in his trench waiting for the downpour of bombs hammering his position to stop, but there is no end in sight. Terrible explosions shake his surroundings and he spends more than two hours praying and crying, asking God to save his life. There is no enemy to shoot down, no one to be seen, only falling bombs.

Unfortunately one of them has fallen too close, the explosion has thrown him out of the trench and now he is lying on his back with his abdomen completely ripped open. His guts are sticking out and part of his intestines are on the ground beside him.

The pain is enormous, he is losing a lot of blood, he is getting dizzy and going into convulsions. Because of the cold his limbs are freezing. But he can't move. Maybe he also has a spinal cord injury. He doesn't even know this but it has also happened, he is paraplegic from the waist down, the only thing he knows is that he can't move an inch or his guts come out even more.

Lying in the snow stained with blood and guts, he spends hours without moving with explosions near him, which fortunately or unfortunately do not reach him. He lies there until he loses consciousness completely. The bombing stops, he regains consciousness, he trembles, his first thought is to remember his family and his home.

He has a slim hope that someone will come to his rescue, but as time goes by, death draws nearer and nearer and he will not make it through the night if someone does not come to his rescue.

After long hours of terrible suffering, screaming unanswered, with no hope of being rescued, suddenly the sound of armored vehicles is heard. Our soldier looks around him in the dawn light, he has awkwardly recovered his sense of sight with the light of dawn. The horizon is clearing and he can see his surroundings more clearly. What he sees is desolate, no one has survived of those who were with him. They are all in pieces on the ground. His companions are literally broken into pieces, an arm here, a head there. He is the only survivor of the bombing.

Finally an armored vehicle is drawn in front of him, but, to his misfortune, it is not friendly, it belongs to the enemy. Some soldiers come out, pick him up, and, without further ado, drag him along the ground and throw him into a crater that a bomb had opened that terrible night.

He shouts and begs for mercy, but they pay no attention to him.

Now they are throwing shovelfuls of earth over his face, and, little by little they are covering him up, until finally he is buried alive.

He has no more strength and can no longer scream or move and is suffocating as dirt enters his mouth and nose in his desperate attempt to breathe underground. As the earth is thrown on top of him, he feels that he is suffocating more and more, he squirms as much as he can to try to get out of there. Dirt gets into his wound and it stings terribly. His last thoughts before the darkness descends are for his wife and small children. The dirt has already entered the wounds, now he can't breathe, move, or do anything. It still takes about two minutes of suffocation and agony before he finally dies.

What was it worth being there for? What greatness is there in this death?

Meanwhile in Milan his wife is safe with their two children. Just the night the bombing started, she, tired of not knowing anything about her husband and giving him up for dead, decides that it is time to turn the page and free herself from all the tension of this war. After having suffered a lot, after months without news of her husband, that very night, she has a date with a handsome Italian boy who comes to pick her up in a nice car. They go out to party and during those hours she finally enjoys herself a little and forgets about the war and her husband. About the same time that her man is dying in the crater, she goes to bed with the Italian and for a few moments forgets everything she suffered.

Shocking narration, isn't it?

Well, the lesson of all this is that what the fuck are wars!

Some will say, what a woman! how bad she does these things!

I will tell you what I think. This woman **is not bad,** we should not hate this woman, nor should we criticize her, nor should we despise her in the least. She has also suffered a lot, not as much as he has, but she has also suffered a lot. Circumstances have been like this, the death of her husband has coincided with the day she was able to enjoy herself a little.

No one should hate her or women in general. It is life itself that is hard, she who has already suffered the unspeakable, is in her right to enjoy herself a little. If she could she would have been by his side, if she could, but she could not.

The lack of information meant that, despite having him constantly in her thoughts, she decided to turn the page, at least enjoy that day. She thought it was almost impossible to return to live with her husband, one day she had to give him up for dead and this was the day.

That's how hard life is, women are neither bad nor good, they adapt to what we are. If we are very good they compensate by being bad, if we are very bad, they will become very good to compensate. It's a kind of coupling, adjustment, whatever you want to call it.

That's why you shouldn't think that hating them will make you stronger, on the contrary, life is hard, not them.

We should love everyone, the good women and the bad women, because there really are no bad women, women are like that due to adaptation to the environment. We must be above good and evil and be **the invincible man** who is not affected by anything, who never suffers, who adapts to everything, who does not make excuses, who does not complain, who does not look for scapegoats to accuse of the evil in the world.

The only one you have to beat is yourself.

The invincible man improves himself to become more fun, more cheerful, more unconcerned with things that don't matter. He becomes hard as nails, to such an extent that nothing affects him. The betrayals, the deep disappointments that life gives us, do not affect us at all. The invincible man loves himself and does not let anything or anyone make him feel bad.

The invincible man had only one enemy, his previous version, the serially programmed version which he defeated. Now he has no enemies, he has himself, and, also the whole world to enjoy the wonder of life.

Even there buried alive, the invincible man feels at peace with himself, without hatred or rancor.

That's right, sometimes this happens, sometimes they send the invincible man to battle hell and he comes back decorated and in perfect health.

The trauma of the first girlfriend.

The first bride is the one that gives us the biggest shock of our life. We come to her totally innocent and good. We come believing in love and that we have found happiness. We care absolutely nothing about our alarming love behavior, which is driving us headlong into a tremendous emotional dependency. When the day of the breakup comes, the world comes crashing down on you. That day is the worst day of your life. Everything you had believed in, collapses, everything you had fought for, you lose, everything you thought was going to be eternal, unconditional and immense, is taken away from you. Many do not get over it and are traumatized for life, or with major psychological problems. Some become sensitive, others contemptuous of women.

This love never comes back, because you will never be able to give yourself as much as you did with this first girlfriend. So love, if it exists, happens in these few years of youth, where you really believed in love, you were reciprocated and you had moments of great happiness with that girlfriend you thought forever.

The harsh reality shakes the boy and anxiety crises, depressions, melancholy, shits, sometimes lasting years, sometimes months, sometimes a lifetime, can occur.

This first big blow brings you back to reality, and shows you that only a few women will be very kind to you, and for a limited time.

In reality this love is an anomaly, something that only happens in this juvenile stage, and not always, only with the few super kind women that are still out there. Women to whom, you will no longer value so much or give yourself so much if they appear later, because of this initial trauma.

After this you can fight for love again, which is what happens most of the time, only to take another setback much faster but less painful; or directly, harden.

The normal thing is to be erring and erring for quite a long time, until finally, around the age of 30, you have adapted to the interaction with women and you stop suffering.

This does not mean that that first girlfriend is bad, far from it, she is good, good within this anomaly in which they are good with their partner. As I said before, they are neither good nor bad, it depends on how you are; if you are good they will be bad, if you are bad they will be good. In this case the guy is innocent and good and this anomaly occurs, and so, being good, she behaves quite kindly, but, finally, the adjustment occurs, and your kindness is repaid with abandonment.

You are also partly to blame for this breakup, because you end up getting bored of the quiet life that this woman gives you, and your detachment from her is initially paid for with more love, but, little by little, the girl hardens and a distancing on her part takes place, until the final breakup.

Let's not complain, complaining is for losers, women are the way they have to be.

They are the ones who change us from soft, dependent and unmasculinized, to tough, tough guys. **Be thankful for every woman who leaves you,** because it will make you tougher, more attractive and stronger. In the end you end up becoming an invincible man if you endure everything and overcome everything.

The best woman I know.

The best woman I know is a really kind woman for her environment. She loves animals, she has a lot of dogs, she also loves cats, she takes loving care of her son, she cleans her home, she is accomplished at work, she is nice to people, friendly, charming and talkative.

A wonderful girl except for the little moments when she gets her wire twisted and turns nasty, this only happens when you do something she doesn't like.

This nice and sympathetic woman who produces sympathy for her wherever she goes, separated from her husband. Despite so much sympathy, she did not hesitate for a second when she took away the villa he had been building for many years with his effort. She also took away his son and trained him against him to such an extent that the son does not want to carry his father's surname. She also took away his car, in short, the one who was her beloved husband became her hated enemy.

This has to make you reflect on how they are. When you are "the man" they are good, but if you let them down they will take revenge for all the time they think they wasted with you. Time they could have spent with the real man, someone else who would have treated them better, or at least not disappointed them so much.

This is the nicest woman I know. Is she bad, no, it's the way it has to be. When you get them involved in something like marriage, the more involved they get, the more they will make you pay for it later. When they decide you are no longer "the man", you will pay for it at a hugely expensive, crazy price! That's the way things are, and that's the way we have to accept them.

This is the best woman I know, dangerous to those who fail her, nice and friendly to those who fuck her, unless you are the husband and let her down.

This woman is thrilled with me and calls me regularly to go around with her, but since I don't get fucking shit involved, nor do I get her involved, I don't let her down either, and so I can be hanging out with the beast without her attacking me.

A seducer is a tamer, a master in seduction is a daring tamer who knows how to handle the situation with temper and impose himself. The master of seduction is always a brave man, a hero, because he keeps women who behave like real wild beasts at bay. There are many of them and they hardly ever attack him, and when they do, he knows how to defend himself. The most.

Those with whom you go have destroyed many men, now they are meek and docile before your fucking power. They are also submissive to your fucking cock, but that only lasts for a while, and since you can't fuck them 24 hours a day, sooner or later you'll have to put up with the wild beasts again, trying to kill you.

Every tamer has his whip, it is used to impose himself and make himself respected, you also have yours, no, it is not the dick, that is not enough to tame them, the ultimate weapon is called "the dark seduction".

If the tamer hesitates, if they see weakness, they eat him alive.

Masculinity.

I have written entire books dedicated to masculinity, so it seems that there is nothing more to tell on this subject, but that is not true, there are more things to tell. The truth is that we men have lost masculinity due to the loss of testosterone. In fact, the men of the 70's of 75 years old had 800 (don't ask me what measure it is) and the men of today of 25 years old have only 550. This masculinity is lowered by the industrial food products that we are forced to eat in supermarkets. Go to measure it to the tribe of the jungle of Papua New Guinea and see how much it gives.

Another part of this loss of testosterone comes from the fact that the jobs we do no longer require physical strength. In the old days, all jobs required physical strength.

The warrior, the porter, the farmer, the hunter, the mill worker, the fisherman, the builder, everything was done by hand. People had testosterone and were strong and macho. Now it is not like that, now we have the computer programmer who moves the index finger on the mouse, we have the writer like me who sits down to talk and the voice recognition program already writes for me what I say, no need to write, we also have the civil servant, who the only work he does is to go to the workplace, then he sits there for eight hours and goes home. There are almost no jobs that require physical effort, and therefore, this masculinity is lost.

Music is also important, nowadays there is nothing but reggaeton with autotune that you can't even understand what they are saying. I have even heard Gregorian chants of monks with autotune, what is this? Meditation mix? It's a laugh. There are no rock bands anymore, there used to be rock bands with really tough guys, real rock stars.

That is why this masculinity must be **exercised.** Lately I've been noticing blacksmiths a lot, these people build their knives and swords in their home forges. These men are really tough guys who make works of art with their hammer and forge. This puts on muscle, the heat also helps to slim down, it's an activity that seems to me to be super macho.

There are also musical groups that are like a throwback to the past, super masculine guys out doing Viking and Nordic music. These guys come out bare-chested walking through the snow with axes, dressed like Vikings, practicing fights and playing drums.

Drumming is a tough guy activity, a very muscular and warrior type. The drum is the most empowering thing, that's why the Arabs took them into battle, they called them "war drums". With their roar they intimidated the enemy.

An invincible man always hears tough guy music and of course drums. Besides empowering you with its sound, it also helps you to get into trance, a fierce and warlike trance.

The Scots seem to me to be really tough guys, as well as the Russians. In Scotland there are a lot of bands that play bagpipes, rock guitars, and a huge amount of drums, which brings you back to the tough macho of yesteryear.

Clothing.

This is a bit of a controversial topic, because the normal thing is to want to maximize your options to seduce girls by dressing very well and looking very attractive, with jackets, suits, expensive clothes and good shoes, also perfumes and accessories. This is good and it is true that it gives more power, but I don't follow it too much. I like to make things difficult for myself, that's why I especially look at guys who are very badly dressed, but who project strong masculinity.

It seems to me that the more poorly dressed a guy is, the less he's trying to please or seduce them, he's happy with himself and doesn't give a fuck what anyone thinks, including women. Dressing poorly is a real tough guy thing to do.

To be always dressing very handsome, is a little softness, which denotes that you do not have the total power to seduce girls by yourself, or at least, you have doubts, and therefore, to make sure, you have to put on all kinds of complements to feel attractive. When you're super powerful, you're dressed any way you want and you're attractive. You can be attractive dressed in a dungarees up to almost the neck with nothing underneath, or walking in flip-flops on the street, or in shorts, or in a swimsuit, or in any way, like the American redneck.

It is true that this will close doors for you with very superficial women, women who are, so to speak, posh, who go about being fine, elegant, but even some of these women may like you if you become a muscular, defined, strong and macho guy.

If you feel your fucking power strongly you can dress how you want, even go barefoot in the street and they will see you as masculine and macho. You will scare them a little, because they are not used to such security. You don't prepare for them, you are the important thing, you and your comfort, they don't condition the way you dress.

This is why I think that the seducer who dresses as he pleases, who wears a mechanic's overalls, who wears a grease-stained suit, or a suit from the construction site, or from painting the house, or from raising the cement-stained wall, is more powerful than the one who wears Armani.

If you are involved in very fine environments, (eh producer), I recommend that you dress fine to be integrated in that social group, because being badly dressed would produce a quick rejection, but, once seduced, they must also see your masculine side, the tough guy, your version as a mechanic who fixes the car, as a careless man who has not shaved today, as a powerlifter doing weights. They should also see in you a scruffy male, who will be less handsome, but more masculine. Some will like this version better than the branded version.

If you're already attractive dressed in any way, what would you be if you dressed well? something tremendously powerful.

So to sum up my thoughts, I say to you that always being badly dressed is wrong, because you yourself minimize your chances excessively, but always being well dressed is also wrong, because you show excessive interest in pleasing and liking them, and that is a weakness. A real tough guy is muscular, often dresses the way he wants, and still attracts women.

Elimination.

Many brag about how many girls they have picked up each year, and go around bragging about their successes. Well, that's initiation level, when you become a master of seduction you don't brag about the ones you pick up, you brag about the ones you eliminate, about all the abusive and mean ones you've managed to remove from your life. You brag about not suffering the terrible, unpleasant and constant nuisance they create with their complaints and demands. Your fucking power thanks you because you respect yourself, and this increases it.

Eliminate toxic people from your life is your obligation: that friend who disappears, that lover who is too demanding, that one who pretends to abuse. They are better out than in, you should not communicate with them at all. The only possible communication is to discharge them for their disappointing behavior. In addition, the reason for their removal is explained to them, so that what little conscience they have left, they will be shaken. Pure dark seduction.

Good women are acquired happily and eliminated neither happy nor sad, maybe a little sad in some cases, but quickly happy, knowing that you have done the right thing, and excited, because you have the time to make new acquisitions.

Bad women are acquired by being sad and eliminated by being happy. They are acquired by being sad, because even though you know they are going to give you problems, you have to add them up. This is dangerous and you only do it on the rare occasions when you feel like a seduction junkie, and, although you know how problematic they are, you acquire them anyway. This is a weakness, you need to flirt so intensely, that you even acquire women that you know are bad. In these cases when you are really happy is at the time of elimination. Most of the time you're smart and you're not even going to seduce them because of their huge and clear badness.

The production process is like this, in order to be able to eliminate at will, you must first acquire. The success of the year is quantified in terms of the girls you have eliminated, not the ones you have acquired.

These eliminations are huge triumphs in the case of bad girls.

It is much more masterful to eliminate than to acquire.

Some good men.

There have been many men who have been tremendously damaged in their interactions with women and also by life itself. These men have one common characteristic, and that is that they have tolerated abuse and have become dependent on others, people who have no life for themselves. This weakness of character is detected by interested women who come to them to take advantage of them. The weak, the soft, do not know how to say the magic word, "no". Everyone abuses them. Thus, little by little, they lose self-esteem. They end up being pessimistic and defeatist with themselves. They visualize a future of failures, which unfortunately, will materialize much stronger than they imagine.

Some end up in the geriatric ward at the age of 53, others frequent psychiatric hospitals, others are social stinkers who have no friends, no social life, no ability to relate to anyone, and remain in their homes, locked up until their death. Others become overly misogynistic, others depressive. Many of them take refuge in religion as a way of salvation. The religion that will lead them to a better life. They are waiting for the next life because they consider this one as lost.

Some bad women.

A bad woman is a blessing. It is a blessing because she is really unbearable, and after a little contact with her, you immediately become disgusted with her demands, abuses, and bad behaviors. The good thing is that thanks to this we will have the perfect excuse to leave her, she gave it to us.

They are worthy of elimination and they know it. When we leave them we have already taken our good sexual benefit, but not even thinking like that, only in the sexual, it is advisable to continue with them, because the damage they cause with their abuses is very large, so they should not, can not, and usually do not last.

The only thing they are good for is to increase our number of conquests. They are numbers, fucking numbers, we don't even remember them, they are really insignificant.

Get this woman out of your life fast, it will make you powerful. You will be anxious to dedicate yourself to your production, because this has been fucking shitty. A bad woman if she falls into the hands of an invincible man, is a good woman. These are our market, the ones that make it possible for our production to be massive. An invincible man is grateful that these women appear.

It puts them in place, enforces respect and rebalances the system.

Some good women.

These good women, kind to say the least, are very difficult to get rid of, they are always doing good deeds, showing affection, understanding, they put up with everything, and they don't leave no matter what you do. This is a very big problem.

They are there waiting for you to slacken your production, crouching to hunt you down, they are always available. In the end they end up attaching themselves to you because of their extreme kindness and it costs a lot to get rid of them. They don't do anything bad to you, and that's the problem, they weaken you little by little, some of them can trap you. That's why, if you don't want to have a serious and formal relationship, picking up a good woman is bad.

The most important chapter of all the books.

I have called this chapter "the most important chapter of all the books," because I think it is really the most important chapter of all the books I have written. I think if you are not a mystic, a person with concerns beyond the earthly, you will probably find this chapter horrible. I know, I know I am a seduction coach and this is not what is expected of me, but I am something more than a coach, but after explaining all this in a deep way, I will be quiet and I will not say any more mystical things.

How to materialize what we want?

In the book JD Absolute Seduction I explained the layers in which your head must be segmented. In the book "how to materialize what you want with the fucking power" I explained how to materialize, but I did not put both together, here I am going to do it.

I will explain things from the origin, however mystical and strange it may seem, down to the most superficial thing in the world.

Beginning, in the astral plane, in the other dimension, there is an infinite energy charged with love and peace, this energy, this infinite power, you can call it God, you can call it the universe, I have called it the fucking power.

Well, from this dimension that we imagine to be an infinite ocean, a kind of funnel rises through which small parts of the fucking power change dimension and enter the physical world. This fucking power creates a materialization, a being, that being is you. It does this because it wants to experience the physical world through you and all beings.

That's why we say that you have the divine spark inside, and it's true, you are part of the infinite fucking power.

Here in the physical world you go about your life not knowing who you really are. The natural laws of attraction make you start liking girls and you want to get them. You read seduction books and things that stay on the surface, without getting to the heart of the matter, without giving all the answers. In this fucking chapter we're going to get to them, you'll see.

So the years go by, suffering and enjoying this physical world, until one day, through meditation, or deep relaxation, or simply going into a trance, with music, with a drum, or just spontaneously feeling something deep inside you, something suddenly appears, it is a vision, or rather a sensation most of the time. In that instant somehow, you are aware that you have this immense power.

This is the hardest thing of all, to connect with the other side, to be aware that you have the fucking power, and not only to be aware that you have it, but to feel that you are the fucking power.

This is something that most people never achieve, and so they live their entire lives without knowing who they are and without feeling the fucking power.

You who have already felt the fucking power, even if you don't fully understand it, know that there is something beyond you, a higher self, an energy, something infinite.

In my case, for example, I was aware that good things would certainly come into my life. This happened to me while listening to a song, at that moment I felt an enormous power that I did not know where it came from, nor did I know anything, but I did know that everything I wished for was going to manifest.

Over time by reading mystical books you realize that this crucial moment, this small enlightenment, this awareness, is the starting point for whatever we wish to have in our life.

Then, later on, years later, going even deeper, you realize that you are nothing more than self-aware, manifested fucking power. You understand that you are not really your physical body or your mind, but self-aware infinite energy, aware that it is manifested on this plane.

From then on everything is much easier, then when you have become aware of who you are, you realize that what you used to call divine help is not such, because it is not something external to you, but you and the fucking power are one.

The first revelation is.

"Me and Fucking power are one."

That is why everything you focus your attention on will grow, will grow because of the enormous power that your fucking power gives you.

Those who have made it this far use their fucking power to create whatever they want, a play, a sculpture, a building, a car, whatever.

The second revelation is.

"I am the invincible man."

A man who has the fucking power with himself is therefore an invincible man. He is a man who, whatever he concentrates on, will succeed.

Now I am going to focus on seduction, as superficial as it may seem. So, you are already aware that you are fucking power manifested in this plane, therefore you start to externalize this power in what you want, as you want to be a seducer, you ask for help to the fucking power to guide you on what you have to do, and the first thing it tells you is: "I want to be a seducer".

"I am the best seducer".

So the third revelation is.

"I am the best seducer".

How can you not be if you and fucking power are one? The fucking power manifests itself by saying "I am the best seducer" and you really are, because you have the power of all the seducers of all the epochs of humanity. You become aware that you are a highly seductive man, the best.

Then you think that others are not aware of this fucking power, and that many times because of this feeling of emptiness and envy that they have, they will attack you. Therefore you, who from pure fucking power have materialized into an invincible man, dictate the following phrase which is the fourth revelation and goes like this.

"I make myself respected."

How you want to make yourself respected in seduction and in everything in general, that's why little by little, with experience, dark seduction emerges. It emerges as an adaptation, as a defensive weapon, as an armor that protects your two deepest identities: the invincible man and the deepest of all, the fucking power manifested.

This dark seduction arises because we receive many attacks, envy and complaints.

Besides the fucking power tells you that you are superior. Although deep down we are all one, not everyone is aware of who they are, so here on the material plane you are superior. Superior because others are not aware of being fucking power manifested and only vibrate at a very low vibration.

They are usually underneath in their awakening, they are in an ocean of superficiality disconnected from their fucking power, that's why they are underneath, and if they are not, you apply the dark seduction and put them underneath. You put them underneath because only then they will see you powerful and they will really like you, because only then they feel your fucking power that impresses them. This comes from the times of the caves where they were attracted to the strong man, the one who defended and protected them from dangers. Therefore, to really attract them, they must see you above them. Therefore, the next thing that emanates from the invincible man is this fifth revelation that goes like this.

"I don't value them."

You should not value them because in this world kindness is paid, excessive valuation is paid with contempt. This happens because of ancestral genetic issues of the caveman that did not treat them excessively attentive, it coincided that this strong and macho type was the one that best protected them, so they associated this strong and macho type to their survival and that is why even today this criterion governs their selection. They prefer the toughest and meanest man who values them little or not at all. This has nothing to do with mysticism but it is also important.

The next thing the invincible man does is to emanate masculine qualities well. Once we have defended our deepest identity with dark seduction, we have protected our manifest and conscious fucking power and our self-concept as an invincible man. Now we show the part that emerges from the dark seduction, the nicest part that manifests first of all is a very masculine body and mind, therefore the emanation that comes out of the invincible man is the sixth revelation that says.

"I am masculine."

This attracts girls and they like you without the need for any seduction methods. You have an alluring essence that emanates from deep within. You are happy because you are the fucking power that manifests itself in an invincible man, you use the dark seduction with which you are protecting yourself from all attacks, you have masculinity.

Now you feel joy, charm and charisma, being aware of all your power, therefore what the invincible man says now will be two statements in which one is a consequence of the other.

"I am the charming scoundrel." And therefore

"I am cheerful and fun."

To be the cheerful and funny charming scoundrel, you just have to follow the rational methods that I have invented as a result of my field work and attentive observation. They are methods created rationally but have a deep emotional and mystical base, because they emanate from the joy of knowing that the fucking power and you are one, and that is why it is very easy to develop what people finally see: the jd method and the el edp method.

With the jd method you will be fun, uninhibited, carefree, comfortable, complicit, and shameless if necessary.

With the edp method you will be the distant and dangerous star that performs these actions

Fun, uninhibited, carefree, comfortable, star, kind-hearted.

As a result of this long process of meditation, awareness and experimentation, it will happen that what you are concentrating on, the girls, will materialize.

Girls will appear, girls who like you and are easily seduced by you. These will be the materializations that you create with this whole process.

Now comes the most mundane part, and that is, of course! nothing will materialize just by thinking. This will help a lot, but it will not be enough, **you will have to practice on the field,** so that all this mental work can really manifest. The more mental work you have done, the easier it will be to materialize your fucking power and turn it into victories, and the less suffering you will suffer. Still, despite all the mental work, you will have to go through a long and hard learning process on the playing field. The more fucking power you feel, the more quickly what you see in your mind will materialize in your actual physical interactions. This will be the part that will require the most time, the part of realizing in the real world your interactions.

The more dedication you put into it the sooner you will succeed, the more fucking power you feel as a result of all this mental and spiritual process that we can also call the internal game, the easier it will all materialize, you need both parts.

The internal game, the visualization is nothing more than establishing a connection between your physical self and the ocean of fucking power. This will produce a kind of double funnel that connects the two realities, through which the fucking power flows into the material world,

This fucking power after this inner work, or inner game, will produce these materializations that we call pickup girls. In order to fully develop your fucking power you must meditate and visualize yourself in your successful role with the mental screen. That's why visualization is so important, that's why visualization looks like magic, because you really do magical things.

And this, my friends, is the explanation of everything, of how from the most mystical to the most material.

Whatever we want to manifest must be done as in this process, feeling the fucking power and channeling it towards what we desire. Thank you for listening to these mystical words.

Now I will only talk about the invincible man and seduction.

Exterior
Soy alegre y divertido
Soy el sinvergüenza encantador
Soy masculino
No las Valoro
Me hago respetar
Soy el mejor seductor
Soy el hombre invencible
Yo y el Fucking power somos uno
Meditacion y concienciacion
Esencia
JD y EDP
Dark seducción
El hombre invencible
Fucking power materializado y consciente
Conexión
Exterior
Soy alegre y divertido
Soy el sinvergüenza encantador
Soy masculino
No las Valoro
Me hago respetar
Soy el mejor seductor
Soy el hombre invencible
Yo y el Fucking power somos uno
Meditacion y concienciacion
Fucking power infinito

Meditation to feel the
fucking power.

I know I said before that I would not talk about mystical things anymore, but I have forgotten about meditation to connect with the fucking power, so I apologize and tell you this, promising that this will be the last mystical topic I will deal with.

To feel the fucking power well we have to put ourselves in a state of deep relaxation. We will achieve this by playing a rhythmic and relaxing music, breathing very deeply and slowly, with our eyes closed, sitting in a relaxed position. Then, when we are very relaxed, we will visualize a white light coming out of our chest. This light is our fucking power that surrounds us and gives us power.

We will stay like this for half an hour at the most, breathing, listening to relaxing music, and seeing this white light that surrounds us. This creates the connection to the infinite reservoir of fucking power. The double funnel will become wider and more fucking power will enter us. With this stronger connection to our fucking power we will be able to materialize much more easily what we want, as we will have much more.

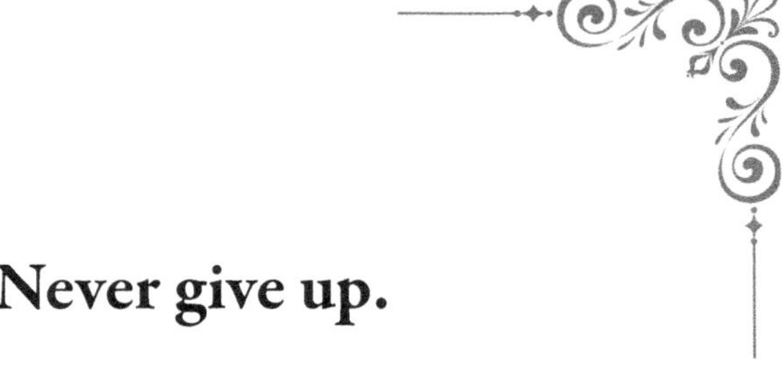

Never give up.

An invincible man never surrenders. An invincible man is like the Spartans, there is no escape, no surrender. When he sets a goal he goes for it with everything. That is to say, with all his fucking power. He concentrates on that goal and does not stop until he achieves it, no matter if he has to spend 50 years sacrificing and giving up a lot of things in his life, the invincible man never gives up and continues fighting until his last breath.

Another characteristic of the invincible man is that he never complains, the invincible man knows that everything falls on him. He is sent to war and does not complain, he is falsely accused of any shit and does not complain, because complaining is weak. The invincible man assumes his responsibility, that burden is his burden, be it just or unjust. Later he will fight that accusation or that action that discriminates him, but at first he bears it without complaining.

No matter how difficult things are, no matter what happens to him, the invincible man never complains about anything, he is always happy, he always takes action to restore justice; because the invincible man is a righteous man who seeks the good.

Whoever does evil to those who do evil is actually doing good, so as I said in dark seduction, doing evil also does good. In addition a very great good, the balance is restored.

The invincible man has his criteria and rewards and punishes according to them.

The invincible man is like the Spartans, there is no retreat, no surrender, no shirking of responsibilities, the invincible man fights and dies if necessary, without complaint, assuming his condition as a man, and even more as an invincible man.

Like the brave man that he is, he sets out like Don Quixote to undo wrongs, but he is not mad, the madmen are all the others who seek to do away with the invincible man.

The invincible man is the soldier who died in war, the discoverer who discovered and explored continents, the builder who erected the pyramids, the inventor who invented a machine, the governor who administered his province, the Indian who defended his territory, the seducer who seduced women.

The invincible man and love

The invincible man believes in love, but in a good love, not in a love corrupted by need and weakness. The invincible man can have hundreds of loves because none will cause him much harm, he is strong. That is why a seducer is an invincible man, a man who, no matter how many relationships he gets into, never gets excessively damaged, and if he gets damaged he recovers easily, because he is strong, because he knows who he is, he is an invincible man.

In the end love grows if you have **presence**, that is if you suddenly feel the present moment as if time stops, you also need to be **aware** of what you are living. Sometimes without realizing it you enjoy love unintentionally and by chance and it is beautiful too.

You know it could end at any moment and you are prepared. They are moments, sensations that come and go. A smoke that sometimes becomes liquid and remains a little longer. They are also good things that you take from this life: the pleasures felt, the sensations experienced, the illusions. Love is 90% illusion and 10% real. It is the illusion that you have to feel it. If you are a little stunned you will be able to feel it too. You know that pain can and most likely will come, but you enjoy sometimes these moments too. After this love passes, if it passes, which is what happens in the vast majority of cases, you will be damaged for having felt it, this time you will lose by a beating in this game.

The invincible man and death.

Suddenly one day someone unexpectedly leaves and you didn't even have time to prepare for it or to say goodbye. This leaves you sad and saddened, because you realize that life goes by so quickly that you don't even notice it. That's why you have to take advantage of every moment, because we don't know when we will leave. No one's life is guaranteed forever, we will all die, even the invincible man will die.

Other times it is not death that you meet, but a serious accident. This accident could have happened with a motorcycle, or with a car, a fall, something fortuitous. It may also not be an accident, but a financial or emotional setback, a blow to your life that you did not expect. Perhaps you are very deserving of this because you risked too much, it does not matter, we never regret it. We will call it an accident.

The fact is that sooner or later this accident can happen and you have to be prepared as well. The invincible man leaves his things well organized and whoever comes after him can continue his legacy.

If the accident is not very serious, the invincible man takes advantage of it. So he can empathize in the hospital with the nurses who take care of him, for example, any time is good to establish relationships with beautiful girls. Even if he is in pain, the invincible man keeps his attractiveness intact.

I remember when I had an appendicitis operation when I was 18, I was very thin and I could hardly walk except by holding on to the walls, because the surgery hurt me. Some girls came to see me and were impressed by that feeling of vulnerability, seeing me weakened must have awakened in them a maternal instinct of protection. The fact is that they all said that I was more attractive than ever. In a hospital convalescing from an operation you are also attractive and you are an even more invincible man.

If an invincible man finally dies, that person is lost, this is bad, but even worse is the fact that his knowledge is lost. The invincible man treasures an infinity of wisdom, and if he does not leave it in writing, all those experiences are gone and no one can access them.

That is why invincible men are cautious in this case and leave everything written down, they leave their memories, their experience of life, and thanks to this they never die, they are remembered and admired long after their death; sometimes centuries later, sometimes millennia.

The invincible man remains in the heads of those who knew him, in their memories, in their books, in their videos. The day the invincible man dies is the day the myth is born and becomes immortal.

Transcending seduction.

The invincible man masters seduction totally, and this is already so easy that he looks for new things in which to stand out, so he can become rich, be famous, or do daring actions and various adventures. The invincible man has infinite self-confidence and nothing can take it away from him. Neither sickness nor pain nor the problems that may appear take away his confidence. The invincible man does what he wants, is accountable to no one, has fun as the most, and respects his own rules, not others, he rules his world. And since he lives this way: cheerful and carefree, this increases his charisma, because girls see him differently from all the others, he does not worry about pleasing, or being handsome, or anything else, he only takes care of what he wants.

The invincible man no longer applies dark seduction, because that is for people who are affected by what they do. The invincible man goes on his way because they don't really do him any harm. The invincible man doesn't suffer or get angry. He already knows how they are and accepts it. The invincible man is always happy, he never complains. He will accept whatever comes to him, he will live his life exactly as he wanted, he will not be attached to jobs, people or anything.

He enjoys playing the organ, going on a trip, or flirting with an attractive lady, or perhaps a pretty young girl. The invincible man rules his life and lives it the way he wants.

Evil.

Today those in charge are abusive and profoundly bad people, they play the good guys and call us, the invincible men, the ones who fight injustice, the bad guys. So translating this, we the bad guys are the good guys, and they, the good guys, are the bad guys.

We are governed by our conscience that tells us what is good or bad, not by what we are told from above. Today the bad guys are the good guys and the good guys are the bad guys, so let's do our bad deed of the day, which is actually a wonderful deed, because it fights the injustice of the supposed good guys.

Women.

A woman with whom you screwed up, a woman who is lost forever, a woman you cannot get back even if you change your behavior a lot. In some cases you can recover, but it is extremely difficult. If the woman has seen weakness, she has made her judgment in a microsecond and discarded you. If you have softened, shown yourself needy, sensitive, overly affectionate, she will not have liked it and now it will be extremely difficult to seduce her or to win her back.

What we must do is to abide by what she says, she doesn't want us as lovers, she doesn't want us to have anything amorous with her, great! we accept that she is the friend.

Now we are going to constantly mortify her with our other flings, probably her friends, probably girls she knows. We enter the friend zone but we don't focus on her, but we have her there as a friend, and we are dedicated to everyone but her. Then we will be in the friend zone but on the high side, we will generate attraction to her to the maximum, because they are always envious of the others, they always want what they all want.

She had it and lost it, now she pays dearly for it, now we give her her medicine, what she gave us before, but, applying it ourselves. Now she is our friend and we are not going to give her any chance ever, that is a punishment, to do what she wanted.

Immiserable, it is never softened, nor is it ever tried to be seduced again in life, it remains there mortified forever, it burns in hell.

We dedicate ourselves to all the others, we always get better than the one that despised us.

When we don't think about them, we don't value them and we don't want to seduce them, when we look down on them, that's when we become invincible men, men who sometimes are generous and concede, but who they don't really deserve. We don't care about them, we don't care about them, we don't value them, we don't admire them, we don't see the sexual side of them, we only see nonsense and conceit, we only see their problems. We are above all that, and we only show a neutral interest in those we see as more kind and fun. We never go after any of them, if we get them fine, and if not, there are more, we never give them the satisfaction of rejecting us. When you collect the piece it is because it was totally delivered. Sometimes if we give them the satisfaction of rejecting us, this happens rarely and we don't give a fuck what they do or say.

In reality everything is a game, we have a good time and we have lots and lots of conquests because we don't give them too much importance. We give importance to ourselves and to our fun world.

The invincible man in you conquers wherever he goes without worrying too much about this issue. For you it is something normal, a favor you do them, because you are kind and you want them to be well. And if to be well you have to sleep with them, then you sacrifice yourself. Poor things.

Invincible man phrases.

Indifference punishes more than revenge.

Many times being tough means playing soft.

When you confront a girl is when she starts to value you.

Invincible men do not tell what they are doing, they tell what they have already done.

That girl you think is good is the one who will hit you the hardest.

Whatever happens to an invincible man is just what he needs.

Invincible men cannot be defeated even by killing them, because their free spirit will always remain.

The invincible man is often a legend, and this legend comes precisely because he only cares about enjoying himself.

Never try to reason with a woman.

From them you can expect nothing but: betrayal, lies and false promises.

You have to live day by day like Rambo, every day adapting to the changing environment.

There is no such thing as love, love went away in childhood when we stopped being children and our mother stopped paying so much attention to us.

It is more important to enjoy than to add up.

To add up to a lot, you have to be calm and happy.

The invincible man does not care what they do to him, it is as if he were not himself.

It is much more masterful to say no than yes.

Self-demand is good for growth, but too much of it is a weakness, because you worry too much about it and therefore give it power over you.

Everything that worries you has power over you.

He who cares for nothing, is above everything, nothing can affect him.

Don't worry about showing who you are, she knows who you are better than you do.

The bad guy doesn't go around bragging about being the bad guy, he knows what he's doing.

The bad guys are the good guys, the good guys are the bad guys.

In reality today the bad guys are really the good guys. Those who call themselves good are the bad guys.

Every day you can reinvent yourself and be a new you better than the previous one.

Sometimes you have to destroy the old self, sometimes you have to reform it, it always needs a little change at least.

They call us bad guys, we think we are bad, but we are the good guys.

In the game of love, men have been the losers since the beginning of time.

In love you can't win, at best you can't draw.

Fucking power creates a layer of protection over us and we get out of big problems unscathed.

Behave as if you were not afraid of anything.

Behave as if you know you cannot fail.

Today is your best day.

Fucking power guides you.

Ten tips to govern your life

1 Don't seek people's approval.
    2 Work on yourself physically and mentally.
3 Don't justify what you do.
4 Demand excellence in what you do.
5 Do not chase women.
6 Create your own source of income.
7 Work to achieve your dreams.
8 Set high goals.
9 Do not accept companies that distract you from your mission.
10 Reward yourself for your triumphs.

The brutality of men.

We men have been stabbed, stabbed, sabered, thrown to the bottom of the sea, shot, had our heads cut off, electrocuted, shot, blown up, crucified, and a lot of other barbarities; and that has not been done by women, we have done it ourselves.

We men are the enemies of men themselves because we are so savage, and in spite of all this, here we are!

Man's life is very hard, man is the one who had to bring money to the house, the one who had to emigrate and leave everything to support the family, the one who went to the sea to fish, to the forest to hunt, the one who faced the beasts.

We are wild! and that is how it should be, you should not repress your masculinity. We have survived everything, especially ourselves, which has been the most dangerous thing for us, and here we are, another millennium inventing ways to go to Mars and advancing science.

It's dangerous to be a man, but you should be proud to be one.

Pain.

The invincible man tolerates pain, and not only tolerates it but even likes it. When an invincible man is suffering he knows he is on the right track. Nothing worthwhile is achieved without great suffering. Except with women with whom we do not have to make an effort and they practically come to us, in everything else we have to suffer and we have to have a hard time to get what we want.

Many times shortly before achieving success comes the worst moment. A terrible moment when it seems that it will not be possible to achieve our goal. A moment in which normal men give up, this is the moment that we invincible men are waiting for with illusion, because we know that success comes later.

When everything goes wrong, when the effort of many years goes down the drain, when all the work done seems to have been for nothing, that is when success really comes. When we go through this tunnel we know that the exit is coming soon and that a blinding light awaits us.

It is very hard to sacrifice, to make an effort, to work from sunrise to sunset on something, to put all your effort into it, and to see that not only do we not get closer to our goal, but we get farther and farther away. But this is what usually happens just before the triumph. Just as the sea withdraws when the tidal wave arrives, everything we have achieved is unjustly withdrawn and we suffer great pain. Then all that is taken away is returned to us a hundredfold, so rejoice in suffering, and even more rejoice when you do not get what you want to get, it is coming. Be glad when your efforts are not only not rewarded but punished, that is the moment when victory begins. A job well done is always rewarded. Midnight is when the new day begins.

Sex, sex, sex and don't forget the violence.

As the master Marilyn Manson said in his song "This is the new shit" translated, "This is the new shit" sex, sex, sex and don't forget the violence. What's up? of course we do, we invincible men like sex and we practice it as much as we can with as many as we can. Yes, sometimes we are a bit obsessed with it too and want to try new positions, new activities, or just enjoy the perversions we can think of. So what? Well of course we do, thanks to all this perversion the species reproduces, couples are formed, people are met and life moves forward. Because yes, fucking, you meet people, it's good for relationships. Most of the time these women you fuck are not worth much as people, but sometimes they are nice and apart from the enjoyment of sex, your culture increases, because you learn things from them. There is always someone who knows how to make a special food, or knows a place, or has an interesting hobby that you then incorporate into your life. By becoming a great womanizer you will acquire a great culture and you will learn a lot of things. We should not feel at all ashamed of liking sex, on the contrary, we should be very proud of it.

As for violence, what can we say? Fantastic too! We men are up to our eyebrows in testosterone and we can not be quiet leading a sedentary life from home to work and from work to home, we have to do intense physical activities where we can develop our: strength, competitiveness and if necessary even violence.

Let's not forget violence, it makes us masculine, we make ourselves respected with forcefulness, and most importantly we respect ourselves by making ourselves respected. A violence generally in terms of defiant or combative attitude, it is not necessary to go around hitting each other, but if it were necessary to defend oneself, it would also be done.

Let us not forget violence, it led us to defeat the cave bear, to kill the mammoth, in short, to survive in cave times. Intelligence, cunning, strength and violence created this world.

An invincible man is usually peaceful, but sometimes he has to endure abusive situations, which require his dose of violence. Then you bring out your inner caveman, your jocker, and teach him a few lessons.

There are two types of lessons:

- Flying
- Nailed.

The flying lesson consists of hitting from the bottom upwards and then it flies away and as I said, you put it to fly like in "IT".

The other variant is the dive lesson, from above you hang on it and hit it downwards, thus lowering its height until you reach the ground where it stays stuck and quiet.

Both choices are good, the flying ones allow for more show, but are harder for him the pinning ones because they require several blows to screw him to the ground.

Yeah, sometimes it's more satisfying to put a jerk to flight than to get laid by a hot chick.

Yes, as the illegal said -I'm a punk, I'm a tacky guy and I also go at full speed on the road.

You can't be defeated even in death.

It happened once that a warrior killed another warrior, cut off his head and carried it by the hair, displaying it before his terrified enemies. What this warrior did not know was that the one whose head he had cut off was an **invincible man**.

Severed heads sometimes have a few seconds of consciousness and may move their mouth or eyes or grimace.

This enemy with the severed head already dead in a few moments, but still alive, had a glimpse of consciousness. He knew he was a fucking severed head and he could see or notice his enemy next to him and what he did was to bite him with all his might on one leg. Yes, the freshly severed dead man's head bit the victorious enemy.

And do you know what happened? This wound became infected and as it was in very ancient times of the Middle Ages, this caused a general infection that ended up killing him.

Before dying the warrior who had cut off the head said -defeated by a dead man1-.

That's right my friend, even after death you can win; sometimes the triumph comes when centuries have passed since your death and you are given the recognition that you were not given in life. Other times these strange things happen, like what happened to the warrior who was bitten by a head.

That's why you can't be confident either, if you have defeated your enemy you must finish him off so that he doesn't rise up again, or it could happen to you like it did to this warrior.

The truly invincible man needs only one second to win.

So it is in kissing, so it is in life.

One second of precision and you claim that new victory.

The invincible man is addicted to victory.

What the invincible man likes most is to succeed in what he sets out to do, to defeat his enemies, to rise up, to win, to be the winner.

Therefore, he has strong competitiveness, predatory instinct, absolute confidence in his abilities, capacity for sacrifice, faith in the fucking power, and certainty that he will achieve what he sets out to do.

The invincible man does not hesitate, he does!

The invincible man achieves his goals.

The invincible man assesses the situation well and does whatever it takes to succeed.

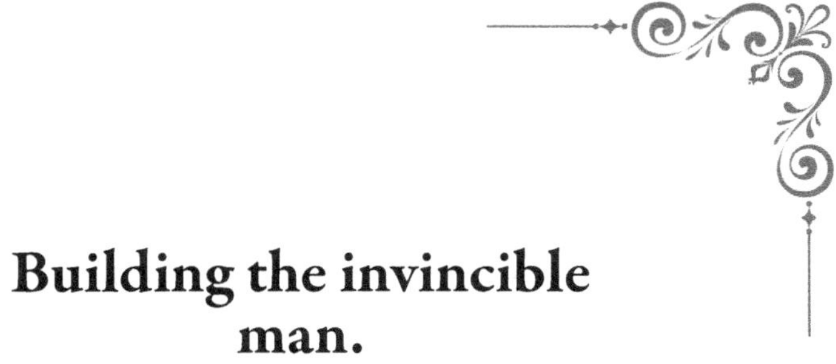

Building the invincible man.

The invincible man is built with the mind. Reality is a matrix where you live in your own reality. You build this reality yourself and it affects you and conditions your whole life. You receive what you think you deserve, you submit to the laws that you create for yourself. You don't really exist and this is not reality. That is why there really are no limits. Read Jacobo Grinberg and his "Synergistic Theory".

You and the fucking power are one, you twist reality in your favor, because the reality that you see is nothing more than a convection that you accept, it is what you project with your mind. If you think differently you will project a different reality. The fucking Power is in you and in all things, you must activate it by believing in it, believing that you have it, that you are one with the fucking power. Meditate, let the mind go blank. Look at the white light.

Then miracles will happen, everything will be possible. That's why you have to be aware that you are an invincible man.

The invincible man faces any challenge. The invincible man never gives up. In fact, the more difficult the challenge, the more motivated you will be to overcome it. The invincible man wants difficult challenges, challenges that require him to improve himself. Doing normal and easy things is not motivating.

Where others are afraid and do not try, the invincible man dares.

The invincible man takes risks.

The invincible man goes through life cheerful and carefree, as if he will never die, or really doesn't care.

The invincible man never wants to do anything, he always does what he finds interesting, even if it is risky and difficult.

The invincible man faces his fears, he is just and good, he gives out joy, happiness, and love; because in the end you can get love. By becoming a person who puts aside hedonism, puts aside enjoyment, then you could become someone who gets love, because the invincible man gets this too if he wants to.

Nothing and no one can stop the will to succeed of an invincible man.

Invincible man statements

To finish the book I am going to put some affirmations to repeat in your fucking head every fucking day until you have incorporated them and they remain there giving you the power to become an invincible man, a divine being.

If they don't like the way I am, fuck them!

I am what I want to be.

I cared about me.

I am the best.

Fuck the neighbor.

They're going to send their fucking mother.

I do whatever I want.

I feel good.

I like to be me.

I love life.

I enjoy.

Here and now I am in the present moment.

I focus on my target.

Whatever the Don Nadies say, they won't fuck with me.

I will succeed regardless of whoever it may concern.

Yes, I'm a womanizer, what's wrong?

I am proud to do what I do.

I am proud to be who I am.

I admire myself.

No one is more important in this world than myself.

I only have me and my fucking power.

I am invincible and not even killing me will defeat me.

Even in defeat I am still invincible.

I am up for any challenge.

I improve all aspects of my life that matter to me.

I can achieve absolutely anything I set my mind to.

My faith in myself is absolute.

I trust my fucking power.

I trust my fucking power.

I have what I want.

My life is wonderful.

If my life is not wonderful, I build it wonderful.

I am not going to do anything to please someone I don't like.

I liked myself.

I set ambitious goals.

My passage through this life will be remembered.

Whether they want to or not, they will have to listen to me.

I am here to do good.

Sometimes doing good means doing evil.

I am very happy doing whatever I have to do.

I enjoy everything immensely.

There is no punishment I cannot bear

I am full and perfect.

I transmit positivity.

I am positive and attract positivity.

I am fucking power manifested.

I have the power.

Remember that you have the most powerful weapon in the universe, a weapon that will always protect you, lead you on the right path and give you infinite power. Be aware that if you develop this weapon well, you will win everything you set your mind to. You believe in your infinite and divine fucking power, which you increase with meditation and awareness. When you and the fucking power are one, everything is possible.

Shackleton.

Shackleton was an invincible man who set out with other good guys on an adventure to explore the South Pole. His ship became trapped in the ice and was eventually so imprisoned that it was completely destroyed. He and his entire crew were isolated in the frozen sea and survived by eating seals, and even played soccer. The morale of the whole expedition despite all the setbacks was very high, they knew that they were led by the mythical Shackleton and they were totally confident of returning home.

Shackleton planned his escape from the ice and together with a few others embarked on a boat bound for Elephant Island, where whaler bases were known to be located. This island was at the singular distance of a thousand miles from their position. A single degree of error in their course would have thrown them far off course and they would not have seen it. But they were not discouraged, so far they went, they advanced across the ocean, paddling at times.

There was a tremendous storm that almost sank their boat. Incredibly they reached Elephant Island. But at the point where they arrived with the boat totally destroyed and irreparable, it was a point where there was a great mountain range that stood between them and the whaling bases. It was very high and totally impossible to reach, it was an impossibility. But for an invincible man like Shackleton this word did not exist.

Without delay Shackleton set out to climb those mountains. After a climb of 27 consecutive hours, they finally reached the summit. This feat of climbing those mountains without any preparation or means was considered one of the greatest feats in the history of mankind.

There at the top, after months or God knows how long, they finally sighted a small village. They went down and told their story. Soon all the men were rescued by a whaler. Thanks to the steadfast determination of the intrepid captain they all returned safely to their homes. Franco Battiato sang it in an excellent song.

I saw this in a documentary in the hemisferic of the city of arts and sciences in Valencia and I was amazed.

Yes, Shakelton was an invincible man. One of the most important feats in the history of mankind was done by this man, who showed a capacity for survival and will to live above any obstacle.

Let this serve as an example as an invincible man.

Exercise to become an invincible man.

To become an invincible man, nothing better than to value your physique and your mind.

Physicist.

You work on your physique by doing all kinds of exercises: sit-ups, push-ups, running, aerobics, strength, whatever it takes. You do it to look good. You also go on a diet and you don't stop until you have the perfect body that will allow you to achieve your maximum performance. I don't know much about this so you'd better consult experts.

The mind.

You must visualize yourself as the invincible man facing the most difficult situations. You must in that dangerous or scary situation behave like the invincible man you want to be. You do this with the mental screen going into relaxation. After doing this visualization you become aware that you are already like that and behave as such.

Then in real life at all times you are aware of being the invincible man, the winner, the one who cannot be defeated or being defeated. You feel invincible like the Porsche 911 turbo RS pulling out of the curve, like the Kind Tiger tank in World War II that took out 19 enemy tanks single-handedly.

Bruce Lee in the fight, Casanova in love.

You have better weapons than others, you have something overwhelming, and you manifest it in your world. You crush all problems and difficulties.

You have maximum self-confidence. Take this as an example. There was a Brazilian player of Valencia CF in the late 90's called Viola who said the following sentence.

"If I control the ball in the area, with certainty, it's a goal!

Now that's a phrase, that's certainty, I still remember it and I put it here as an example.

This is how you should be, if you have the opportunity, you will certainly materialize your triumph.

It is not enough to win, you have to overwhelm.

The invincible man is characterized by his awareness at all times of his unlimited power.

Life is hard and there are many difficulties but if you are aware of being invincible in times of difficulty you will not give up, you will continue fighting totally unconcerned about your current situation; because you know that eventually you will win, because you will never give up, because you are invincible and who is invincible wins.

Men's lives are especially hard, much harder than women's, and we don't complain about anything, we hold our heads high, we look ahead and face a new challenge, because we are men, the best of creation! and nothing and no one can stop us.

Feeling like the invincible man.

Everyone could be an invincible man, but only those who feel their fucking power intensely can be invincible. In every time and place there were invincible men who did legendary things. There are now and there will be in the future.

You must feel special, different from the rest, called to great things. You are aware that you have an infinite power within you that can convert and shape your whole world as you wish.

You can overcome all difficulties and achieve all your goals because the fucking power is with you.

You look, breathe and feel the power in you. You are happy because you are invincible, whatever you focus on you will manifest. You create your life and enjoy it.

You carry the power of all invincible men together in yourself.

You are the Spartan at Thermopylae.

Shakelton climbing the mountain.

Magellan crossing the strait of Tierra del Fuego.

Casanova conquering.

Vivaldi composing the four seasons.

Alaric conquering Rome.

Sometimes losing and many times winning, you are the invincible man.

Long live the invincible man!

The world is waiting for you, invincible man! Go conquer it!

Let's play!

Did you love *Invincible Man*? Then you should read *The Failure of Love. The Trap of Serious Relationships*[1] by John Danen!

[2]

Love fails, relationships break down. Sometimes the worst torment is that these dysfunctional relationships do not break and you live in hell. That's what this book is about, how a toxic relationship hurts you and how to get out of it.

---

1. https://books2read.com/u/b5lLxp

2. https://books2read.com/u/b5lLxp

Also by John Danen

Seduction 5.0
S.A.X.
Chicas complicadas
Seducción 5.0
El libro del tonto
Macho Alpha
Macho alpha extracto
La seducción después de la pandemia
Terriblemente atractivo
Seducción 5.1
Sedução 5.1
How to be Cool and Attractive
Sedução. Avançada. X.
Garotas complicadas
¡Basta de ser buen chico! Sé un chico malo.
El método JD. El método de seducción de John Danen
El arte de agradarte a ti mismo
¡Basta ya de abusos! ¡Defiéndete!
Enought with the abuse! Defend yourself!
Máster en seducción
Las mujeres. El amor. Y el sexo.
Supera la dependencia emocional
Atrae mujeres con masculinidad
JD Absoluta seducción
El fracaso del amor

Entender a las mujeres

La vida del seductor sinvergüenza y encantador.

El arte de la dureza

Terrivelmente atraente

Deixe de ser um bom da fita! Seja um mauzão.

Superar a dependência emocional

A arte de se agradar

Pare o abuso! Defenda-se!

O fracasso do amor.

O método JD

Don´t Be a Good Boy! Be a Badass

Complicated girls

The Art of Pleasing Yourself

Duro y Sinvergüenza

Mestre en sedução

JD Method

The Failure of Love. The Trap of Serious Relationships

Master in Seduction

A. S. X. Advanced. Seduction. X

Women. Love. Sex

How to Become a Real Man. Be an Alpha Male

Attract Women with Masculinity

JD Absolut Seductión

Understanding Women

The Life of the Shameless and Charming Seducer.

The Art of Toughness

Tough and Shameless

Überwindung der Emotionalen Abhängigkeit

Maître en séduction

Schrecklich Attraktiv

Surmonter la Dépendance Émotionnelle

L'art de la dureté

Die Kunst der Zähigkeit

Hör auf, ein guter Junge zu sein, sei ein böser Junge
Assez D'être un Bon Garçon ! Sois un Mauvais Garçon.
Die Kunst, sich Selbst zu Gefallen
Dur et sans Vergogne
Hart im Nehmen und Schamlos
L'art de se Plaire à soi-Même
Das Scheitern der Liebe
L'échec de L'amour.
Meister der Verführung
Die JD-Methode
Maestro di Seduzione
Terriblement Attrayant
La Méthode JD
Capire le donne
Compreendendo as Mulheres
Comprendre les Femmes
Die Frauen Verstehen
Les Filles Compliquées
Komplizierte Mädchen
JD Séduction Absolue
La Vie du Séducteur Charmant et sans Vergogne
Les Femmes. L'amour. Et le Sexe.
Mâle Alpha
S.A.X.
V.F.X.
Donne. Amore. E il sesso.
Ragazze Complicate
Superare la Dipendenza Emotiva
Seduzione. Avanzata. X.
Dark Seducción
Il Fallimento Dell'amore.
Il Metodo JD
Alphamännchen

Atrair Mulheres com Masculinidade
Attirare le donne con la Mascolinità
Attirer les Femmes par la Masculinité
Mit Männlichkeit Frauen Anziehen
Frauen. Liebe. Und Sex.
L'arte di Piacere a se Stessi
Mulheres. Amor. E Sexo.
JD Seduzione Assoluta
JD Absolute Verführung
JD Sedução Absoluta
Das Leben des charmanten, schamlosen Verführers
Smettila di Fare il Bravo Ragazzo! Essere un Cattivo Ragazzo.
La Vita del Seduttore Affascinante e Spudorato
A Vida do Sedutor Encantador e sem Vergonha
Macho Alfa
Uomo Alfa
Séduction 5.0
Verführung 5.0
Seduzione 5.0
Duro e Senza Vergogna
Duro e Sem Vergonha
L'arte della Durezza
A Arte da Dureza
The Fool's Book
Das Buch der Dummköpfe
Il Libro dei Pazzi
O Livro do Tolo
Dark Seduction
Dunkle Verführung
Sedução Escura
Dark Seduction
Seduzione Oscura
Le livre du fou

Como materializar lo que deseas con el fxxxxxx power
Como materializar o que você quer com o Fxxxxxx Power
El ángel Sex-terminador
El seductor vampiro
O Vampiro Sedutor
Sex-Terminating Angel
The Vampire Seducer
How to Materialize What You Want With The Fxxxxxx Power
El camino del maestro
Il vampiro seduttore
O camiño do mestre
La via del maestro
Der verführerische Vampir
Le sedusant vampire
Der Weg des Meisters
La voie du maître de la séduction
Master's Path
Come materializzare ciò che si desidera con il Fxxxxxx Power
Wie Sie Ihre Wünsche verwirklichen können mit dem Fxxxxxx Power
El método EDP
O método EDP
The E.D.P. Method
Comment matérialiser ce que vous désirez avec le Fxxxxxx power
El hombre invencible
The EDP Method
O Homem Invencivel
l´Homme Invincible
l´Uomo Invincible
Invincible Man

About the Author

Español.

Soy un hombre vividor y divertido que busca el lado bueno de las cosas siempre.

Mi experiencia es el campo de las relaciones personales y de la seducción. Por eso tras dedicarme larguísimas décadas a ello, quiero trasmitir mis conocimientos. Para que las nuevas generaciones tengan unos conceptos que les den una ventaja competitiva sostenible y poderosa en el campo del amor.

Quiero ayudarte a a conseguir tus metas.

Portugués.

Sou um homem animado, e divertido, que sempre procura o lado bom das coisas.

Minha experiência está no campo das relações pessoais e da sedução. É por isso que, após décadas de dedicação a ela, quero transmitir meus conhecimentos.

Quero ajudá-los a alcançar seus objetivos.

Inglés

I am a lively and fun man, who always looks for the good side of things.

My experience is in the field of personal relationships and seduction. That is why, after decades of dedicating myself to it, I want to pass on my knowledge. So that the new generations have concepts that give them a sustainable and powerful competitive advantage in the field of love.

I want to help you achieve your goals

Français Je suis un homme vif et drôle qui cherche toujours le bon côté des choses.

Mon expérience se situe dans le domaine des relations personnelles et de la séduction. C'est pourquoi, après m'y être consacré pendant des décennies, je veux transmettre mes connaissances. Pour que les nouvelles générations disposent de concepts qui leur donnent un avantage concurrentiel durable et puissant dans le domaine de l'amour.

Je veux vous aider à atteindre vos objectifs.